# WHY-
# SHAPED
# SCARS

# WHY- ?HAPED SCARS

New Poems by John Wing Jr.

Black Moss
Press
2014

Library and Archives Canada Cataloguing in Publication

Wing, John, Jr., 1959-, author
Why-shaped scars: new poems / by John Wing Jr.

ISBN 978-0-88753-534-5 (pbk.)

I. Title.

PS8595.I5953W49 2014          C811'.54          C2014-900761-2

 **Black Moss**
EST. **Press**
1969

Published by Black Moss Press at 2450 Byng Road, Windsor, Ontario
N8W 3E8. Black Moss books are distributed in Canada and the U.S.
by Fitzhenry & Whiteside. All orders should be directed there.

Black Moss Press acknowledges the support of the Canada Council for
the Arts and the Ontario Arts Council for its publishing program.

 ONTARIO ARTS COUNCIL
CONSEIL DES ARTS DE L'ONTARIO

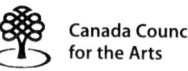 Canada Council    Conseil des Arts
for the Arts      du Canada

Edited and designed by The Wingmen:

Meagan Anderi, Natalie Brander, Kristen Dimenna,
Eliane Drijber, David Fine, Anna Glenn, Sarah Goldstein,
Marissa Lunardi, Stef Maxim, Sarah Meeke, Laura Sorge,
Irena Sziler, Sofija Tesic, Dan Zompanti

PRINTED IN CANADA

*For John Ditsky, 1938-2006*
*and Marie Arthurs, 1910-2009*

*Teachers.*

# Table of Contents

*A sense of humour — a real one — is a rarity and can be utter hell. Because it's immoral, you know, in the real sense of the word: I mean, it makes its own laws, and it possesses the person who has it like a demon. Fools talk about it as though it were the same thing as a sense of balance, but believe me, it's not. It's a sense of anarchy, and a sense of chaos. Thank God it's rare.*

– Robertson Davies

## CHAOS THEORY I

This is what we say to ourselves
out of the world's earshot, we say,
"Oh, to be young again." Or something
unpoetic that conveys it. But of course
it's a lie. We're wishing to be young
with the knowledge of its preciousness,
the ability to say no. To trot back
and flip through ambition's attic,
understanding better what would have
been best. Choke off the words that
cut holes in your parents, when they
were trying so hard. Don't cheat on her,
or her. Or her, you bastard. Oh, to be
young again and smart as Jesus.
Even though the real wisdom age
brings is a relief map of the pure
capriciousness of it all. The reason
for everything is chance. The swerving
of a drunken car that obliterated another
neighbourhood boy on his bike instead of me.
And I kept riding, heart-slammed, legs
moving while every other part of me
fought for air. Caught a glimpse of death
that day. Don't think he saw me.

## AT YOUR OWN RISK

Don't swim,
but I know how.

Summer mornings
at Briarwood pool
with a hundred other tots
in silly suits, all slack jaw
and unformed sinew,
lined up for a fat man
who squirted water in our faces
through a closed fist.

We dead-man floated,
dogpaddled, crawled
with stinging eyes
to the holding edge.
I tried to cross the deep end
once, foolish. Foundered
in the center, churning
waves. "Don't panic!"

the fat man called,
too late.

## POST-IT NOTE I

A pink post-it appears
on a turned blank page:
"You should write a poem
about bunnies."

I suppose I should.
Is any poet complete without one?
From Blake's "Bunny, bunny,
burning bright," to Thomas'
"Time held me green and dying
though I sang in my chains like a bunny."

But here's the thing,
a friend told me this:
as a boy, his father would
take him hunting in the winter,
a .22 squirrel gun in his teenage
hands, and they would occasionally
stumble upon a rabbit who didn't hear
them until they were too close,
and it would freeze, hoping
to blend into the whiteness.

His father had keen eyes.
He would point to the quaking
snowball. "Shoot that rabbit."
Small wonder he's a vegetarian now,
wandering lonely as a bunny.

## NOTICED EARLY

The river Styx was said to have
mystical powers. She brought the infant
to the bank, gripped him by the heel
and dunked him, believing it would
make him invulnerable. Today she
would be charged with child endangerment
and sued by his widow for not dunking
the heel too. Foolish woman.

An eagle swooped down, snatched
a wolf cub, then took off again.
The cub squirmed madly, wrenched
himself free of the talons and fell.
Without a thought, the stuttering boy lifted
his toga and caught the bloody thing.
Later he heard his grandmother tell
his mother that it was a sign
that he would rule.

The baby came out of the womb
gripping a clot of blood in his hand.
The father was proud, the mother horrified.
"He will be a Khan," the father said. *He will
bring death wherever he goes*, she thought.
He would conquer half the known world.

Once I scored the winning goal in a street-hockey game.
In overtime, I passed to my best friend from behind the net,
expecting him to score. But as I ran for the front
he passed it back. A first. I hadn't turned,
and the ball got stuck in my feet. I kicked it ahead,
got the stick on it, pivoted, and backhanded it blind.
It went right through the goalie's legs, a perfect five-hole shot.
Pure luck. And no elders watching to say,
"That kid's got *comedian* written all over him."

12

## OLD FACTORIES

The golden-papered soap
catches my eye, and I lift
it for one clean sniff. It smells
of my father's shaving lotion
in the balsa cup, whipped up
by the black-handled brush.

I wonder if fathers
and sons still do that.
Little boys lathered up
and scraped with plastic,
talking of the news
of the day, like men.

# IMMIGRANT

Remembering a boy
from Czechoslovakia,
tossed in our grade four class
in the fall of '68, without a word
of English. The teacher assigned
my friend Carl, who spoke
Polish, to translate for him,
and we watched that year go by
as he became one of us.
A kickball stalwart, a quick,
full-throat laugh, a smile-creased
face I can still see clearly
forty-five years on.

Many things happened that year,
some I recall, most gone, but he
remains: The Iron Curtain Kid,
appearing in the memory-swamp
mist like an oak who set down
his roots before the flood
and grew defiantly tall.

By spring he had some grasp
of non-prepositional English
and small conversations were
available. Last day of school,
always the shiniest of days,
he told us he was moving away.
To a farm. "Mother like farm,"
he said. Carl and I walked him
to his bus. Never saw him again.

## MR. DUNN

Sometimes a teacher pops into your head.
No reason, a snatched phrase leaps from
a paragraph underlined, or some idea he
presented rises and there he is.
Long hair, hip for the time,
stringy and almost flaming red. As red as
orange wants to be. Robert. The other teachers
called him Bob, which was ridiculous.
His first name was Mister.

Forty years since I saw him.
His classroom, first on the left from
the front door. Mr. Dunn: immune to your
excuses. A frown-glare that made you turn
and seek shade. Something about his demeanor
very clearly said, "Do *not* fuck with me."
In the memory I see he's not very tall.
Fireplug short, in fact, but the force was
so potent he could stare you down from below.

For a moment, I'm not fifty-two, treadmilling uphill
to slow the slide. I'm in his class, checking my pulse
for the first time. We're all jogging in place for three minutes,
checking it again, and again after five minutes rest.
He explains what the resting heart rate should be, what
it should rise to while jogging, and how it should equilibrate.
He jogs with us. His heart starts at 63, goes to 130, and then
back to 63. Perfect. Mr. Dunn wins. I still check my pulse
the way he showed us. More often, too.

Now, up by the blackboard, on a saran-
wrapped table, he's placed an entire cow's
stomach. Why do I have to know this?
It's disgusting in a macabre, magnetic way,
like a covered body on the roadside slows
you down just to imagine harder.
And last, Mr. Dunn, the basketball coach,
in a teachers-versus-students game. Maybe
that's where I noticed how tiny he was.


A flashy little guard, ball handler,
behind-the-back passer, great vision.
Here he comes down the lane, left, right,
and up, some tall thirteen-year-old trying
to block him as he pivots just out of reach,
in the air, mind, and rolls the ball
from his hip, heavy spin, off the glass
and in. He falls back on defense,
all business.

# THE BOY'S MARCH

The summer after high school
he worked in a canning factory.
Ten hours a day slapping the same label
on the same can as they rattled down the line
like convoyed soldiers, dressed
in the finest tin-silver, shiny as they
would ever be.

He hadn't considered university,
but after three months, he was
considering suicide. A guidance counselor
said, "You could take a regular B.A.,
that's three years, or an honours B.A.,
that's four." "And then what?" he asked.
"You get a job." He thought, *I've had a job*.

"What takes the longest?" he asked.
"You mean, in years of school?"
"Yes." "Medicine. Medicine takes twelve years."
"Okay," he said. "I'll do that."
She looked at him the way a farmer
looks at a dog who just ate a prize
rooster on instinct alone.

I wonder if he ever went back, after
he took the degree, and looked for her.
Or better, invited her to his convocation.
Would have been a shock, since she'd
probably been dining out for twelve years
on the story of the crazy boy who
said, "OK, I'll do that."

## CATCH

Dad had a curveball, which he called
dinky, but hell, it moved. It would come
spinning out of his hand, and ten feet from
the glove, it would slam on the air brakes,
(you could hear the hiss) and dive down
to the right. It wasn't hard to catch
if you knew it was coming.

I was afraid of the ball.
Thick-spectacled, like him, I was
always afraid of things coming at me.
He would try and smile me out of it,
saying, "But you have your glove
to protect you."

He had an easy motion when he threw.
His arm would swing around chest high
and the ball would come, generally hard (for me)
and in a two to three foot area. Even high school
pitchers have their skills.

We stood no more than forty feet apart
and we threw. He taught me the proper grip
and the weight shift. He hated that we kids
called it hardball. "It's not hardball," he would
say, "it's *baseball*."

Sometimes he would talk about pitching
and tell the story of the pitch he put too close
to the middle on a guy and he belted it
to dead center, but the outfielder, whose name
he always mentioned, ran back half a mile
and caught it, saving his bacon.

One day, after two or three curves, which
were about all his arm could handle by then,
he suggested he throw me a fastball. I wasn't
exactly keen on the idea but I agreed. He warmed
up with a couple I thought were really fast,
and then he called out, "Here it is."

It buzzed as it went by.
I didn't even reach for it. I knew
how much it would hurt my hand
to catch it. I simply moved a little
and let it go. Belt high. Sizzling
through the air.

We walked in then. He wasn't
happy that I'd wimped out,
but he understood. We all come
to accept our children's inabilities.
He was smiling though, as we reached the house.
"I put it right where I wanted to," he said.

## CARNIVALE

teenage cringing
hand-held girl
hormones singing
long gone world

seaside midway
blink-light dome
heard her hearsay
walk me home

brushed up to me
took my hand
gitchee goomee
boy to man

what she showed me
still makes way
youth so holy
age to pay

modern forage
picking stones
heirloom storage
packed in bones

last-night wandered
lights on shore
tell-tales laundered
young no more

brushed up to me
way back there
no one knew me
at this fair

memory's paint could
slick this down
snake-oil sainthood
card-trick town.

## POST-IT NOTE II

"Here's a fine page for your poem
about cupcakes," she writes. Dammit,
muse, stop bothering me! I'm going to
London to visit the queen.

Stopped for a moment in the bakery
at Harrod's and I took a photo
of a thousand (it seemed) cupcakes
under glass. Meant to send it to you.

Once cooled from the oven, the artist
goes to work with his funnel-painter
and icing-brush. Vanilla-white,
confection-pink, sugar-blue.

Saw some amazing architecture
that day. Passed a restaurant called
Monty's Lebanese Kitchen, and wanted
to go in and meet a Lebanese named Monty.

Almost got tossed from the National
Portrait Gallery for taking photos.
But I didn't buy any cupcakes.
It would have been like eating a Monet.

## THE FAN

She wears the jersey of a player traded years ago.
"I'm still not over it," she says.
Her bag includes water and sunscreen, sunglasses, and
a Tiger hat. She buys a program on the way in.

She keeps score while enjoying
an overview of the entire spectacle.
The lime grass, the statues, the scoreboard,
the occasionally perfect sky.

Her scorecard is full of smiley faces, snowmen, and hearts.
She records the game-time temperature and attendance
and has acronyms for certain plays. SOLC, for instance,
means *struck out looking cute*.

She calls most of the players, "Mister." She never catcalls,
unless the whole section is outraged and she can say
something no one will notice, like, "Oh bother!" or
"A less-than-perfect call, methinks!"

She has seen a home run
take her team to the World Series.
She has seen a perfect game
that was not a perfect game.

Coming to the game as an adult, a convert, she notices things
I miss, like player fashion. "He doesn't usually wear
his socks that high," and "Do you think the players know
that white pants makes your buttocks look huge?"

She will spot an outfielder being bitten
by an insect, usually as an important pitch
is being thrown, the outcome of the game
on the line. She doesn't like insects.

She is one face, one mind, in a sea.
Her eyes are bright, her brain a-click.
She's never caught a foul ball,
but she's ready.

## STAGE FRIGHT

*It started here . . .*

I'm thirteen, stepping on the stage
in this tiny gymnasium
to deliver a speech.
It is 1972.

The audience, mostly my
asshole school-fellows, stare arrows
into me. My heart is on cocaine,
and as I stand there,

I can feel my knees quaking
and I'm positive everyone
can see it. I start talking, and the fear
becomes volume, energy, power.

*An accident, really. I'd never felt
the fear before and it came out loud,
sounding confident and large.
And they bought it.*

We are joined, the crowd and I,
fused in sound and control.
The cheers are deafening (defining)
when I am declared the winner.

So loud it sometimes wakes me now,
windmilling my arms, trying to anger
my blood, find the current my knees once
jolted me into one more time.

*. . . and here we are.*

## THE ADVISERS

I remember being so young I jumped
everywhere. Danced in leaping
entrechats to all my classes, pounced
on women, twirled them to my own music,
ripping pleasure from them, desperate
as a Christmas-child.

I ran on my elbows, headstanding
down stairs, swinging on ropes and vines,
naked to every tower window.
To break me, my teachers warned
my parents of the cost of the child
living in my head.

This led to long sofa-lectures on
report card day, which taught me
to split my mind into listener here,
and thinker a-million-miles-from-here.
A discipline that became critical
on the stage I found.

An attention addict,
I murder-envied those who
could capture the classroom
with assurance and ease. Those
mechanical, office cubicle-types
who watch me on television now.

My parents told me to finish
school in case show business
didn't work out. They never
said what to do if it did.

# THE PRESS

That summer, at the bottom
of a lot facing the river,
I worked at the press
of a small weekly newspaper.

I was low man, earplugged
and overalled, standing at
the far end of that grinding,
impossibly complicated ink-monster.

Red, green, and yellow goop-triangles
troweled into the cylinders, truck-wheel-
sized paper rolls fed in and mangle-folded
as typeset information was pounded on.

And the sound, the grease-grind of gears,
which the veteran printer's devils never
seemed to notice, talking loud, nodding
loud, using a blue-collar sign language.

At the far end, the ad flyers slithered out,
and we shook them smooth, turning
and setting them on pallets to be taken
and inserted somewhere, like dildos.

Lunch outside in the sun, eating with
black fingers it took a year to get clean,
the boss would stare at the river and talk
of the boat he was building to sail away.

## SMALL MOMENTS

I shall avoid the many "ifs"
that accompany a surprise love
coming late in the season, when one is sure
the last butterfly has been glimpsed.

I shall not idly spin scenario with
fantasy in my many alone moments
when she comes to mind: her snowy skin,
her flash-flood-green eyes.

I will await another city, preferably
one with a river where we will walk
and be in love with each small moment
rippling by.

## APHORISMIC

Love is, like religion,
peculiar to its adherents.

Luck is air currents
conducting cloud concertos.

Ego is a mirror
I can't see myself in.

Talent is a monster-brat
screaming for food.

Success is what I want
without knowing what it is.

## ESCAPE-PROOF

Mother's uncle was a pole-vaulter,
and back then the pole wasn't springy
fiberglass, and the landing area
was a dirt-pit. Briefly world-class
at university, he was a big man on campus.
One night in 1926 he and a boxer friend
went to the theatre to see a magician.
Knowing the stage manager, the boxer
got them backstage to meet the famous
conjurer, because he'd heard the fellow
had a challenge that any man could hit him
in the stomach as hard as he wished. The boxer
had a corking right hand, and he knew
the magician would feel it.

There are many versions of what happened next.
In biographies (fifteen by a current Amazon count)
some have the great man lying down, others
standing. All agree he took the howitzer shot
before he was ready, and after doubling over
in pain and shock for a moment, gathered himself,
set his stomach muscles and allowed *another*.
The boxer was impressed. To quote from
the first bio I read, at age ten, "his stomach
felt like an oak plank." The first blow, of course,
ruptured the great man's appendix. Peritonitis
set in, and he died within a week.

Some of the books mention the boxer's name.
Others just refer to him as the young pugilist
from McGill University. No one mentions
my great uncle. He's just " . . . and a companion."
But he was there, and this is a piece of knowledge
that makes me wish I could carry the knowing
back to a time we were both alive. Although,
remembering him and our encounters murkily,
he might have just said, "Yeah, I was there.
So what?" Men of that generation were more
accepting of chance. How genetic ability led
to friendship that led to witnessing inescapable fate
strike Houdini before he was ready.

## TEXT ME ISHMAEL

Who stood waving at the dock
the morning the *Pequod* put to sea?
Not Ahab's widow, or Starbuck's
sweetheart, but surely there were some
kerchiefed ladies, maybe even a child
or two, waving as hope shrank, praying
small prayers.

I travel in shorter bursts, go-and-return
so often it unregisters. Goodbyes mumbled
in sleep, returns only noticed by the dogs.
Can't sleep the night before departure,
or the night of return. I pace the house,
counting the bookcases, waving hello or goodbye
knowing I am soon to be taken by a fair wind.

## THE UNDERCOATING

When the real mysteries
have been solved,
(Easter Island, dinosaur
fossils, why people
like yogurt) scientists
will become itinerant,
like dustbowl Okies,
tenured drifters, examining
washing machines and dryers
to prove the single sock theory,
then moving on.

Conversation is a theory,
blogged about
like a bad painting
on *Antiques Roadshow*.
Insured for a song.

When the last answer
is given, and there's nothing
left to know or learn through
experience, will everyone
be together or alone?

## CHAOS THEORY II

The obsessed old man,
rich beyond Monte Cristo,
in plain rags, guru-bearded,
six-inch fingernails scratching
every insane itch, was asked
how he got there, and replied,
"I just sort of drifted into it."
That's right, God's grand design
is a hobo with his thumb out.
You may be exactly where you're
supposed to be, but you'll never know
why you're supposed to be.
In fourth grade, my academic peak,
an admiring teacher told me
she could see me getting my PhD
at twenty. A fine, encouraging woman,
though a failure at prognostication.
At twenty I would drop out of college
to begin my education.

## POST-IT NOTE III

Her note says, "Your poem about kittens
could be written here."

The problem being that kittens,
though adorable, grow into cats,

to whom I'm highly allergic.
And all the neighbourhoods I ever

lived in had that one lady whose
home was a litter box for forty-odd cats.

And she knew all their names,
which still makes my skin crawl.

But I'm getting off topic. Yes, kittens
are lovely when they need you,

like the first blush of a naked girl.
But someday she'll realize you need her,

and then she's a cat and the gleam
in her eyes is ownership.

## TOO LATE

For months she lied;
said all was well
when she knew.

Too many balls in the air,
one mistake in the pattern
and the crash came, all
directions bouncing.

A small time-bomb.
Ticking in a mailbox.

Perhaps her first guilt-wake,
guilt-walk. Every moment coloured
in the screaming mirror.
Hard to focus.

You have to stop and sit down
sometimes, the roar is so loud.

And she's still so young,
years away from

*Fuck it. Let it come.*

# THE MORLOCKS

Driving in a dream,
out of control, almost awake
when a boy appeared,
mouth open, frozen in a second
of light, about to die.

Then I was sitting, choking
on breath, trying to cough
the image away. My wife made
coffee, and after I told her,
asked, "Did you know him?"

I thought before I spoke,
which is unusual. Of course
I knew him. You know everyone
in your dreams. Or you've
seen them. Or they're you.

"A friend?" she asked.
I shook my head, his leering
face burning in me
like a cross. Not a friend.
From that far back? No.

"Maybe you could find him
on Facebook," she said. Is that
the point of Facebook? To hunt
down ancient bullies and write
*fuck you* on their timelines?

You're damn right it is.
The Internet is a time machine.
We travel back and exact our pound.
A leftover, how-long-has-this-been-
in-the-fridge vengeance.

So that's who you married,
and this is where you ended up.
Do you still have the dreams
where you know everyone, or you've
seen them, or they're you?

# JUDGEMENT

In the mirror,
I saw an old man.
Saw the cheek-sink contour
that will be impossible
to hide in ten years.

Saw the lines
deepening into
permafrost-frown.

Shaving with my
reading glasses on,
looking without looking,
my father appeared,
not smiling, not happy.

Wondered if my children
see me the same way.
*Not me, brother.*

# EYES ONLY

lazy music drifting
through windows like smoke

a green rustling of planet-air
through sunburnt trees

the sound of belated greetings
a birthday passed unremembered

a medical report on the table
read twenty times already

memory full and spitting out pages
the huff-sigh of the printer in your head

# THE GILDED CAGE

If I have nothing; if the piles
of bought books and cars and lawns
and trees I foolishly imagine
owning turn out to be nothing
but ideas, what then? Shall
I buy an indelible name-stamp
and brand the volumes that litter
my house? Carve my name in the grass
with horse and plow so it can be seen
from the sky?

What is ego if not denial?
Of death, of time's indignities,
the loss of large pleasures
to be replaced with smaller, safer
ones. The horrible discovery
that real knowledge comes too late,
and thus armoured for the final
battles, one is stuffed with desire
to be dumb again. To love without
knowing pain exists.

See the old man with his concubine
in your youth, and scoff at his frailty,
the smear of wealth that buys her.
Easy to think. See him now and know
it from your own mirror, leaning in
close with an eye-dropper, gulping
pills and perfume to mask the flaccidity,
the skank-smell, the reality that after
the glow wears off there is nothing,
and it will have to do.

## HOME

At a certain age,
all the girls
I wanted in high school
lose their allure.

Girls who sprouted breasts
and new attitudes overnight.

I still have time-travel
fantasies, bringing
knowledge and celebrity
like a bullhorn:

*I have come to fuck you.*
*Please form a line.*

Visiting brings back little now,
because home is not
a place. It's a *was*.

A beach where
the sand was too hot
and the water too cold.

A shortcut between houses
now bricked up by new owners.

## SHOW #8,021

I step up into the light as my name
is given. The host leaves and I am alone,
being stared at with anticipation. As I make
my opening remarks, I look around at those
visible in the side-glow, judging shoes
and hair. The first laughs come and my
brain goes on full mechanism-timing,
gauging the nuance of each sound, suggesting
expression-tilts and inflections to lengthen
or shorten each one.

In the front row there is a woman
sitting alone, the seat beside her
conspicuously empty of man or beast,
and as I march into major routine number
one, and the laughs begin to paint the room
with pulse, I recall that she told the first
performer she was recently, happily divorced.
Around joke number four she smiles
for what I perceive to be the first time
and it dazzles me for a marked second.

She is my age, possibly a year or two south,
her hair a blondish white, and she regards me
with a face that is both pretty and infused
with soft-lit kindness. The sort of kindness
that would show excitement or pleasure
if she saw me nude, perhaps. And now
I am speaking nakedly of the ravages of age
upon my body, and she laughs enough to make
her breasts shake ever so slightly under
a blue and white sweater.

My brain pinwheels its way
through the next few minutes,
combining gesture with step,
turn with pitch, and this woman,
with a delicious roll of middle age
around her center continues to laugh,
and smile, and the part of me,
the small part that's allowed to think
independently while I perform,
starts to fantasize.

So while I briskly paddle and whip
through routines about my daughters
and their schools, their teenage obsessions,
their dating and driving habits, turning
panoramically to give everyone a good look,
I hold longer on her, an infinite half-second
to register reactions and stockpile images
for the dream, now in full glory as she shyly
removes her blouse the way Apollonia did
in *The Godfather*.

And now my wife enters the show
as I speak of marriage and how it relates
to true happiness, and my fantasy divorcee
laughs and shows her expensive teeth, as I
speak of the woman I sleep with while
imagining sleeping with the woman I'm
speaking to and neither has any idea
of the compartments, the many tiny
compartments, the keyholes filled with
laughter and scattered clothing.

As the K-sound words (cold, composite,
indicative) drop like stone-splashes,
we float down the river of my act,
she is holding me, whispering, "It's ok,"
as she rocks me into child-sleep.
The last routine comes slowly, no rush.
Unlike the fantasy, this one is well-built
and builds well. And now the laughs crescendo
into applause and I am warm twice.
Say goodnight, Gracie.

## THE AGES OF SIN

Today the customs booth, the immigration line,
is my confessional.

Citizenship?
Canadian.
Where are you going today?

To Hell, Father.
Remember Jesus Christ your saviour.
Trust in him and confess your sins.

How long were you out of the country, sir?
Four days.

It has been four years since my last confession.
Really, my son?
Okay, fifteen. Fifteen years.

Anything to declare?
(I declare myself President of the state
of confusion and the King of low self-esteem)
No, sir. Nothing.
No alcohol or tobacco?

Have you been touching yourself, my son?
Yes, Father.
That is a mortal sin.
Yes, Father. (Do all mortal sins
feel that fantastic?)

Have you ever been refused entry into the U.S., sir?
(Not since before computers)
Not that I recall.

What if you appeared at the gates, my son,
and Saint Peter refused you entry because
you had unconfessed mortal sins on your soul?

Was there a smuggling incident in 2002, sir?
I have no recollection of that.

God sees all, my son. He knows all.

How did you get your permanent resident status
in the U.S., sir?
I married an American woman.

Did you have sexual intercourse before
you were married, my son?
Yes, Father.
(Of course I did. What century do you live in?)
How many times, my son?

Put your four fingers on the pad, sir,
and then step in here, please, and remove
all of your clothing.
All of it?
All of it. Yes, sir.

Did you take the name of Our Lord in vain, my son?
Yes, Father.
(Does this guy have a fucking camera on me all day?)

Please look into the camera for the retinal scan.

One full rosary, five Hail Marys, six Our Fathers,
the next three First Fridays, and an act of contrition.
Thank you, Father.

Pull over there, sir. Leave the keys, take your ID and go inside.

Go in peace, my son, to love and serve the Lord.

Drive safely, sir.

(Exhale slowly, walk slowly, drive away slowly.
Resist the urge to dance.)

## THE DRAGONS

Today is a long journey
to somewhere I can sleep.
I traveled here, through the snow-slapped
passes, road lanes invisible to
the bleared eyes. Opened the window
several times and stuck my head out
into the fast-freeze air. Didn't see
a car on my side for two hours.
No one else has a long journey today
starting from where I started,
going to where I'm going.

The cold kept me awake,
the fear conjuring up green
ghost-figures, or giant black
swallow-circles. I remembered
a drug I took two or three times
that was all false images, and how
those dragons couldn't hurt me.
Made me happy. The signs
suggested wildlife used the road
as a crossing point, but none chose
my headlights to deer in.

## NOCTURNAL ADMISSIONS

I wake up alone,
but not unaware.

It's always a room.
My room.

Sometimes in a hotel, curtains closed
for the sun, which rose hours ago.

Or a ship. Five feet wide by ten feet long
and many toe-dangers on the bathroom journey.

Or our room at home. She wakes much earlier
and steals out. I wake up alone.

Sometimes pain rouses me, and she's there,
always saying, "You should go to the hospital."

And yet each waking is success, even
the dream-shot that bullets me world-to-world,

Breath ragged with transgression,
into the conscious darkness.

## NOW WE ARE SICK

The doctors came often,
two, three at a time,
asked questions about habits.
Travel, sexual, et cetera.
My answers did not satisfy.

In the hospital you are always alone.
Two or three months before, I had
confessed to years of sin. Every
room in our house confronted me
like her eyes. Even the walls were
disappointed. My answers did not satisfy.

Comedians speak of illness as a gathering
of new material. Minor procedures are,
"I needed a new ten minutes." Real death
scares can lead to a whole hour
of embellished true-story.

But the doctors kept coming
because they had no idea what
was covering my body with lesions
and filling my mouth with
unsatisfactory answers.

Yes, I almost died. But does it count
if I didn't realize that? How close
I came? I have only vague images
of the night my fever spiked
and they packed me in ice. A green
ground-sheet that reminded me
of camp. Rising, floating above
the bed. Ice cubes poured on me.
My favourite teacher appeared, shook
her head, moved on. She looked very old.

After days of wondering and bad food,
the doctors decided my disease had
no cause. The why-shaped scars would
fade with time, they said, as they
planted me in a wheelchair and rolled
me home to grow again.

## CHAOS THEORY III

The wrong reasons are very important.
The flashing of some weakness,
a sibling comparison that reflects
badly, but is visible only to you.
Rather than mentioning it and appearing
delusionary, you keep silent, and it pushes
you the right way. False starts are equally
necessary. Garden paths must be trod,
up with hope and back with shame.
You have to be caught lying by a woman
you love to understand how much it bothers them.
And the mechanism, one of many
yet to be discovered in your engines,
moves you on, swallowing fear and other
indigestibles, pushing you up in front
of the next train. Maybe this time
you'll see it coming up the next
fruitless trail.

# A RANDOM RIVER-SYSTEM

calibrate the distance
study the darkness

reality is a show about the sun
the screen burning as the film is changed

the anesthetist is unconscious
the surgeon's eyes look dead

give the baby a name no one can spell
be assured it will be grown into

children have no feelings
adults have no time

## ODD MAN OUT

The only father at Mommy & Me class.
While the darlings wind-up-toy-walked
and learned search-and-destroy
with building blocks, we birth parents
repaired to a room to hear a policeman
speak about child safety.

When he was done, mostly dealing
with child-proofing the under-sink areas,
and not leaving them alone in a car,
something virtually all our mothers did,
he opened the floor to questions.
And every single one, for an hour,
was about child molestation.

How do you spot one? Who should you call?
(His answer to that was, "The Police, ma'am.")
Should we get a second gun? He asked how
many of us had firearms in the home and all
raised their hands save me, and one lady who
assured everyone she was planning on
purchasing a gun any day.

The cop tried to pivot into gun safety,
trigger-guards, etc., but the Moms were
a pack of wolves with a squirming
animal in their teeth. "Is it okay to
shoot a molester if you walked in
on him fucking your child?" asked
a prim lady dressed like an ex-nun.

The cop hemmed a little, and suggested
screaming your lungs out. I kept waiting
for him to mention that ninety percent
of child molesters are related to those
they interfere with, but he never did.
I was reluctant to bring it up myself,
being unarmed.

## MAD HATTER

Yes, I have traveled, spent
some years in crisscross flight.
Gadded about my born continent,
knowing hotels as some know
the brick-chinks in an old firebox.
Travel gave purpose. I must pack,
awaken, away.

Almost all the trips were done alone
and involved little or no exploration.
The few times I stopped to look were cursory.
Glances only. The early summer hayfields
of rural France caught my eye once, but only
I suspect because so many had died there
in the millennia before I showed up.
I pulled over and stood for an hour
in the shuddering calm until the local
livestock began mooing about my sanity.

The grand idea is to always be on time.
To step on the plane, the doorstep, or the stage
at the exact tick of some appointed, anointed hour.
To hurry is to be afraid. To be late, blasphemous.
My daughter, a chronic time-waster, kids me about it.
"You're always early. You'll probably die early."
We laugh, and I think, *well, better than dying late.*
Yes, much better.

# HOMING

I believe everyone has a spirit-city.
For most it's not your hometown,
since so many of us spent a good chunk
of childhood dreaming of getting the hell out.

My wife claims Grants Pass, Oregon
as hers, but I don't think she understands
the idea. It's a place where she was happy,
and felt loved. But that's not it.

It's not where you were happy, or happiest.
It's not where you fell in love in that
irretrievable time when nothing hurt
and you believed it could go on like that.

It's where you feel most at home.
When you arrive, it seems as if
the whole town has come to the station
to greet you. All the signs smiling.

My two well-travelled sisters, both raised
in small-town Ontario, have chosen their cities.
One Rome, one Naples. Our mother's parents
came from there, but got the hell out.

For me, it's Windsor, Ontario, and if
I tell people, they cock an eyebrow,
and look at me as though
I was released early.

My wife has told me, more than once,
to have her cremated and scatter her ashes
on the Rogue river near Grants Pass.
I've imagined it and Googled the route.

## LOVE FRAGMENTS

I

When I awoke,
she was there
beside me, her hand
within my curve.

When I awoke again,
she was gone.
She'd been gone
for years.

II

One image
is a soaked morning.
You exit the car,
umbrella first,
never looking back.
The umbrella is
the same colour
as your sweater.
A black flower,
floating.

## THERE'S A PILL FOR THAT NOW

After forty, strength takes on
new definitions. Could be patience,
or successful resistance to temptation.
(I am the revolutionary, turning
down a single backstage blowjob.
They'll build monuments to my faithfulness.)

The personal irony is bitter,
only understanding the sea's power
as it begins to ebb. Age is a bright light
in a small room in a police station
where I sit, fighting the urge to confess.

Strength of mind, I think.
My mind will remain strong. But
part of me laughs and asks, "Mr.
Strength-of-Mind, where are your
keys right now? What do you fear
less? What makes you cry
besides everything?"

My friends have begun to die in earnest.
I dream of car accidents, fear mistakes,
my neck a tumour-shaped ball of tension.
I can't walk into a room without picking
out a fallback chair in case the music stops.
My real face is no longer in the glass,
and I refuse to believe photographs.

## THE COLLECTIVE WHO

Here and there, I miss you.
Your secret self-hatred,
your word inventions
(*elbowrotic, clandestiny*!),
your thirst for the sugar
of every fruit-lipped girl,
your bony fingers wandering
in some new moisture.

Your disdain, piercing
sometimes, for advice
(*moderationality*).
The way they kept
telling you to shut up,
not realizing the grenades
inside.

Last laughs are private
(*guffoofaraw*)
and only possible
when everyone else
is gone. Some are, and
I miss them, too.

## BUT FOR THE GRACE

Last night in this hotel,
my cigar-redolent room.
A new year begins tomorrow
and I am still alive.

People die a lot in my job,
and they die alone, in hotel rooms
strewn with a week's newspapers
and room service plates.

They die in cars. The worst way being
en route to the gig, since then
all they remember is you
never showed up.

Better to die on the way home.
Then some say, "I saw his very last
show. It's true, man." And you don't
check out being permanently late.

Some drink themselves into
the coffin: hit-head falls, sudden
liver failure. In the last weeks,
their skin becomes lucent, off-white.

Some park their cars on tracks
and wait for the train. Everyone
else's day is ruined. The estate
a pile of questions.

I think I'd turn my head away
as the train approached, though
I've never considered it an option.
And I am still alive.

Some check into a nice hotel, write
an interminable blog-icide note, spell-
check it, then mix up a cocktail
of Gatorade and antifreeze.

We read the blog note and say,
(to ourselves, because we're alone)
I should have *known*. Should have
called. Done something.

The C's, cancer and coronary, take
a few. They waste away or clutch
and go. Our noble profession
is hard on a body.

Tomorrow I'll be flying somewhere.
Tomorrow is a new year, and I'm still alive.
I'll think of something. It's on the tip
of my tongue.

## CHAOS THEORY IV

Look at five people from the same family:
four are successful, one is not. But thirty years
ago you wouldn't have chosen that one
for failure. He was gifted, honour-bright,
going places. You would have bet on him.
Or a comedian so funny he could make you
forget where you were. Twenty-five years ago
you looked over the crop and rated him
number one, sure-fire, can't miss. Today
he's relatively unknown, he wastes patiently
away. On the phone, his breathing is
louder than the occasional one or two
syllable word he can manage.
Who decided? What gives me
the wherewithal, the get-up-and-go?
The last race I won was to an egg.

## HALF-LIFE OF FAME

In Toronto airport, I see a rock star
at my gate. Twenty-some years ago,
we worked together one night in a bar
in my hometown. Having just done
my first *Tonight Show*, I was more
well known. Ten years after our
meeting, he and his band were
the biggest live act in Canada.

I'm still sort of well known in Canada,
but he's iconic. A rock elder statesman.
He stands at the giant airport window,
watching the plane that will take us to L.A.
lurch in. The band sits around him,
twenty-five years on the road as visible
on them as it is on me, if they
were looking at me.

I mention our single encounter,
and it's clear he has no recollection of it,
and he's treating me as a fan, which I am,
and not as a minor Canadian celebrity,
which I also am. His sentences
are clipped and smile-pronounced,
and I quickly get embarrassed and end our
meeting. We all ride coach to L.A.

## THE SOUND AND THE LIGHT

Mike, waiting
for a liver transplant,
sits backstage at the weariest
angle I've ever seen. Speaks
in whispers, words once
impossible to imagine.
"Is my hair all right?"

Tonight we honour him,
and he waits for his intro,
arranged on his sad chair.
His bulk, so imposing, now gone,
though the stare and lip curl remain.
He's even handsome,
in a prison-hunger-strike way.

He seems almost unable
to move, rolling his eyes
at the video clips they've chosen.
But no small screen, or any screen
really, could ever contain Mike.
We've said it forever.
You had to see him live.

See everything he was seeing.
TV crushed him. Made it unreal.
"They're laughing," he whispers as
the video ends. The man with the plaque
calls his name and he vaults from the chair,
striding away, fused and burning, heading
for the sound, the light.

## RESOLVED

I will be thin again.
I will pause in a forest
and be mistaken
for a baby tree.

Cut and de-branched,
I will be a new beam
in the ceiling
of an old museum.

Women, staring up,
will marvel at my
grained texture,
my board-feet.

Once I could wonder
what might be ahead.
Now I know
this is the view.

## FLORA EROTICA

In a floor-length robe,
the colour interpretive as mood,
she drinks coffee from a yellow cup
and reads what used to be called a newspaper.
Her hair, ash-blonde after years of honey,
flows from her head the way
snow on a mountain becomes water
in spring, and goes on a journey.

As I enter, my own hair
in morning Medusa, she points out
the cactus we planted twelve years ago,
a once-a-decade starburster, and the flower,
which will last two or three days, is out,
throbbed in colour, air-dripped, singing.

Neither of us falls
to the cliché – *My God, ten years* – aloud.
It's just one moment of a long
life by a window, contemplating what
we brought and planted here, now tall
and in bloom. She turns, undoes the robe,
and flashes me – natural as rain.

## TWO GOODBYES

Flying home from the old home.
Saw three siblings and my parents.
Did a show in Tillsonburg for a company
that made foam rubber car seats.
Had a private moment with the boss
and he confided that it wasn't good
to live in the same town as your business.
" . . . then you're laying off three hundred people
and you're all shopping at the same Loblaws."
He lived in London.

Took a late-winter walk with my sister
and she told me the reason our mother
stands at the window waving at the end
of each visit (head tucked a bit, right arm
up, hand Elizabethan) is because her
father did the same thing. The last time
she saw him, both of them knowing
that's what it was, he stood waving
two goodbyes.

My brother, from whom I had been
estranged on and off for many years,
was also doing his version of a visit.
One night I was truly unnerved by a bat
swooping around the basement, and he
went back down with me, packing a broom
to my tennis racket, saying later, "Easy to be
friendly when you're trying to kill something."

Did a hometown show for a local Boy's Town-
style charity (last stop before the reformatory).
Had several "betcha don't remember *my* name"
encounters with old classmates and other oddkins
from childhood, noting the vagaries as always.
(She had the drowned brother, the crazy sister.
He had the three gay brothers and the priest.)
We smiled through all we didn't or couldn't say.

Then on a day when the burly young
tattooed man came to give my father
the first of his now-biweekly showers,
and the mid-elderly Italian barber came
to cut my father's hair, fresh from a White
Rain wash, I left, after taking out the garbage.
While Dad had his trim, Mother stood
at the window, small and blue. Waving.

## THE DEVIL AND MS. EARHART

If they'd asked you early,
before the tingle-thrill of the machine
in your hands, lifting up, the ground
receding, you understanding God
and birds simultaneously, what
would you have said?

If they'd said, "Yes, you will fly,"
would that have been enough?
I don't think renown meant
anything to you. Something
that helped you fly, got you
the hot planes. That was all.

In the airfield photos your smile
is tight, dignitary-forced.
Not nervousness, though,
it's *impatience*. Dammit, let's *go*.
I'm tired of obeying gravity
with you rich bores. Goodbye.

Gods make their offers,
and exact their price. Fame dips
down a chart. Yes, you were *first*,
but real immortality isn't
found until you're lost.
I think you loved every second.

Even the last two.

## WHAT I'VE DARED

In high school I was in a band
called Hard Feelings. I played
traps, second fiddle, skin flute,
and the tambourine, while providing
atonal harmony and building tall columns
of amped resentment. We sang about love,
the depth of love, the misery of love,
the special misery of no love at all
(Special Misery was our second choice
as a name), and the double misery
of love you couldn't escape from.

In university I was in a band
called The All-Niters. I played the harp,
the balalaika and the pink oboe. Sang
some smoke-damaged-furniture harmony
and tried to write lyrics when I should
have been studying. Wrote about the war,
can't remember which one, and the government.
Mixed drugs and alcohol (Binge was the
second choice as a name) and penned
classic anthems like "The I'm Mixing Drugs And
Alcohol Blues." Volatile, we split like atoms monthly,
reforming after each holocaust.

In my twenties I was in a band
called The College Dropouts. Actually
we had a lot of names: The Pogey Men,
The Dishwashers, The Frightened Sheep,
DisCourier, Subterranean Homesick Jews,
This Sucks, This Blows, This Really Blows,
The Bagsuckers, and during a brief
punk period, The Menstrual Boys.
I played the spoons, the rain stick, and the flesh
piccolo, taking the odd lead, mostly
experimenting with tantrum-harmonics.
I wrote songs about the universe and my penis,
which were somehow interchangeable. We
did gigs in underground venues for a precious
few. Talked of making an album most nights
before passing out on bare mattresses.

My daughter, sixteen, has a band
called Crazy Ahab. She is pierced
in many places and may already be
tattooed somewhere a father cannot venture.
This morning she and the crew of the *Pequod*
were working out her new song, "Occupy My Ass."
I play sometimes at a little folkie coffee place
on Sunday nights. If you request a singer or a band,
I'll play their most obscure song. If I had a band today,
we'd be The Settlers, Limpy And The Skin Tags,
or maybe The Post-Modernaires.
I still grab the old flute now and again,
but mostly I just marvel at the daughter,
who considers reading *Moby Dick* in hardcover
an act of rebellion.

## PROGRESS *OBLIGE*

Now in the twenty-fourth year
of our marriage, I begin to see
more of her innate perfection.
This was the year she built
a new shower for the half-bathroom
at the end of the hall. A place where
I hated to wash became one I couldn't
wait to enter and luxuriate in. Younger,
we probably would have had sex in there,
which could have been why she waited
to erect it.

The house has a satisfied clutter now,
most things in their place. She still cleans
the day before the cleaning women come,
which I have stopped mocking. She thinks
of something and I say it, which remains
amazing. Learning to love someone you love
is our mission. Vertigo keeps us off the moral
high ground we once shouted from. She now
accepts my continuing festival of quirks,
and I have learned to speed-read the sentences
she can unload in a look.

## OPEN LETTER

Dear young poet,

Read poetry – a lot of it, all kinds.
Memorize some of it.
That way if your Kindle, iPad, iPhone,
laptop, and TV go out simultaneously
in an apocalypse, you'll still be able
to enjoy it and amaze your friends!
Read it all, and please spare me
the horseshit that you don't want
to read others because it will affect your voice.
Your "voice," if you have one, needs
technique and polish. Imagine a medical
student declining to read books on surgery
for fear it would influence his cuts.

And that poem you wrote yesterday?
The one you recited to your girlfriend
while she was jerking you off, and just
before you came you said, "It's the best
thing I've done – oh God, right there."
Well, some day, in your forties,
you'll find it pressed in some old notebook,
the paper age-streaked black along the folds
as you'll be along your creases, and when you read it,
you'll remember what I said. No, you won't.
You'll remember the girl stroking you
and think: *I recite much better poems*
*while being masturbated these days.*

## THE ARMLESS TROMBONIST

Scientists don't look for facts.
There are none. Probabilities are
their meat and muscle. Would you
bet your salary on the the sun
rising in the east tomorrow?
Yes, you would. That's another
thing about scientists. They answer
their own questions.

Sometimes, looking through
a window at an ocean, or the distant
earth, my name floats up as
the fearful *why*, the existential
*what the fuck.*  I'd like to be
a scientist who could easily scoff
at the low probability of there being
a God, an answer, a reason.

I knew a woman whose child was
torn to pieces by dogs before he
was two years old, and I looked in her
face as a boy to try and comprehend
that grief-abyss. When I had my own
children I caught a glimpse of it, but
she was dead by then. She had two
children. The other one drowned.

Scientists use words like *theoretical*,
*protocol*, and *methodology*, which is
really just *method* with *ology* tacked
on for religious reasons. They smile
with great confidence in the high
probability they know more than you.
Much more. They are the adult
embodiment of *show all your work*.

There was a boy in high school who
played the trombone, my instrument,
but he had no arms. Not even stumps.
Worked the slide with his left foot,
and could absent-mindedly scratch his
eyebrow with his right big toe. Other
things too, I suppose. He probably
teaches yoga now.

Some insist an intelligent designer made
the human eye. They point to its complexity
as proof, failing to notice the optic nerve goes
straight out the back, creating a blind spot.
With neither evidence nor willingness
to bet my salary on it, I have looked above
me and asked for help from the air. And
when the air answers, what then?

## AN INFORMAL HISTORY OF COMEDY

I

Two amœbae floating
in a tide pool,
and one says, "So's mine,
must be the salt water."

People say prostitution is
the oldest profession,
but chances are the first prostitute
met the first john in a mead-house.
But there would have been an
older profession onstage.

II

Two Neanderthals
walk into a cave . . .

Before what we know
as language, the imitator
got campfire laughs
with signs, setting up his
"This is Calon Stalking the Mammoth" routine.

The startled men
laughed themselves silly,
because of course it was exactly
like Calon's peculiar hunting
and sniffing posture.

As they cackled,
one signed to another,
"It is funny because it is true."

III

Early subjects included:
What is up with this weather?
Elephants are better than mammoths.
Girls are weird. And the famous
"I shot an arrow into my fucking foot" dance,
which was so popular it became a musical.

The imitator was the first to notice
a well-fed group laughed loudly and often,
while an audience of unsuccessful, hungry
hunters would just stare.

And he also knew that a man who
made everyone laugh around the fire
would never be as important as
the man who could make fire.

Probably several generations
of flame-funny, Cro-Mag dudes
went by before it occurred to one
that he could make a living at this.
Everyone hunted.
Every night there was a fire.

IV

With language came innuendo
and double entendre, and certain kings,
bored with slaughter, employed their
own comedians. Men who wore
pointy-headed costumes, carried
rattling "funny sticks," and only had to
make one man laugh to make all men laugh.

The risks are many with
an audience of one. Suppose
the King had a difficult day
condemning the treasonous, railing
against weak-livered minions.
One had to be careful.

Finding the gold, the special
bit that made him roar
and never failed – the keeper –
was most important.

Intros were important as well.
A snatch of song. A song of snatch.

## INSTRUMENTALISM

The left-handed piano player said,
"Turn that sound upside down."

Childhood horrors, or so
they seemed at the time, return
like a car in your blind spot.
Large, immediate, from nowhere.

Belief so fervent
that when it proved false,
tiny pieces of me scattered
to corners to believe it forever.

The carpal tunnel trumpeter said,
"If I had to choose between money
and fame, I would choose neither.
Or money."

First touches (the forbidden kind),
the way the whole music room filled
with students somehow revolved in
the periphery of her breasts.

Commenting on the colour
of her socks brought a smile,
and you filed that away forever.

The armless trombonist said,
"It's all in the ankle, man."

## CHAOS THEORY V

Change is incremental
if you're paying attention.
Even the chimps locked in a room
with typewriters pounding out Shakespeare know that.
Here, all over here, is my dissipated self.
In my bookcases, musical instruments,
collections of the history of my mind,
I stand ready to show visitors around,
to explain. "What are your poems about?"
she asked. "Me," I said. "What do you talk about
onstage?" "Me," I said. But no one asks,
"How did you come to be here; to be *this*?"
When I imagine being asked, a line
Martin Amis wrote comes to mind:
"Evolution is not the work of an afternoon."
Or I imagine this: a white plastic bag
left for dead in a shopping mall parking lot.
The wind fills it and it flies across a highway,
pregnant with ambition. In flight,
the handles catch the top bramble
of a bush and it becomes a flag
of surrender.

## GRIFTER

Maybe all wounds are self-inflicted.
Allergies get worse every year.
Joint pain from the morning on.

"You sit too much," she says.
"You need to exercise."
She knows everything.

When she doesn't know something,
like a crossword clue, or why she
still loves me, it's confusing, demoralizing.

Still, her confidence is so beautiful,
the stride of her thoughts, going
somewhere, purposeful.

And she *does* know it. Sometimes
she can't find the box she put
the knowing of it in, that's all.

Being wrong isn't scary
when you're not. And it's not
that I don't know things. I do.

It's just that my knowing is not the fixing,
the figuring, or the measuring kind. My knowing
wins prizes among idiots in bars.

Hers keeps the house in working order.
Where I live, in the shadow of her
confidence, a trivia-dwarf.

Of course all wounds are self-inflicted,
and you certainly don't find strength
giving your confidence away.

## OPENING MONOLOGUE

I'm John. I'll be your comedian.
Once again, we will play our dangerous game.
I will talk, and you will laugh.
No, louder than that. And if you don't laugh,
I didn't do my job. And neither did you, you lazy bastards.
When you laugh, you relax your muscles, boost your
immune system, lower your blood pressure,
and load up on endorphins. If you don't laugh,
I'm not saying you'll get ill, but everyone
will think you're a dick.

Laughter is an orgasm for your brain,
and I want multiple simultaneous
explosive climaxes from everyone.
Come one, come all – over me.
For the men, as a supplement to what
you get at home, and for the women,
a treat you never get anywhere from anyone.

I'll be telling jokes. Straight jokes for ninety percent of you.
Gay jokes for nine percent of you. And for the one percent
still kidding themselves: I'm not gay, but I have this friend,
Bill, my soul mate and life partner who I live with. He's gay.
Wow, is he *gay*. We were having sex the other day
and I turned to him and said, 'Bill, you're the gayest
man I've ever met. You're in flames back there."

As some of you have already guessed, that was a joke.
It was an example of the kind of jokes I'll be telling.
I have short jokes, like: I'm a good lover – self taught.
I have long jokes, like: the Harper government.
I have fat jokes: my sister is so fat, once a guy was
having sex with her and he got lost. They didn't find him
for two weeks. I'll be telling jokes about myself:
I'm fifty-three years old, and my body is not what it once was.
My skin has so many tags I look like I'm on sale at Target.
And I'll be doing this because it's my job.

People say to me, "I've always wanted to try comedy, but I'm
just too insecure." And I say, "No. You're not insecure enough."
I'm so insecure that I get gratification from producing a sound
out of complete strangers. And that's what you are. Strangers.
And don't get me wrong. I don't want to meet any of you
personally. I just want to massage your funnybone until you
erupt in the happy ending of laughter, and I get paid.
I want to be your whore. Me love you long time.

As your whore, I'll do whatever you want, baby.
You want me to talk dirty? "Oh baby, you have
the biggest laugh I've ever heard. Ooooh, smack me
with that big laugh of yours. You are so big, so strong
when you laugh. Oh my god, you're making me funny!
You're making me sooooooo funny! Oh my God, I'm gonna
giggle when I tell this next joke. I'm gonna giggle so hard.
Here it comes, baby. Here comes my punchline."

And I'll do it so well, I will give it up so sweet,
that afterward, you'll say to your girlfriend, "Man,
I think that comedian really liked me."
And I did, baby, I really did.
You were the best audience member ever.
The *best*. (Looks at watch.)
Okay, gotta run. Another show.

## Acknowledgements

One never completes a book alone. For this one I must thank my friend Don Coles, who did an early edit and was a voice of reason and encouragement throughout. Those assigned to editing and designing this book did the really heavy lifting here. They tore my book down and helped me rebuild it – a most unusual and edifying experience. One of the most difficult things to do as a writer is to leave your comfort zone. The editors evicted me from mine, by the scruff of my neck and into the muddy street. It was frightening and satisfying at the same time, though not in equal measure at first.

So, to Meagan Anderi, Courtney-Anne Beatty, Natalie Brander, Kristen DiMenna, Eliane Drijber, David Fine, Anna Glenn, Sarah Goldstein, Marissa Lunardi, Stef Maxim, Sarah Meeke, Shawna Partridge, Lisa Salfi, Laura Sorge, Irena Sziler, Sofija Tesic, and Dan Zompanti go my thanks for their hard work, passion, and enthusiasm. Extra props to Eliane, who was the only one besides me who liked the poem "Images Of Saskatchewan," which did not survive the final cuts.

Special thanks to Marty Gervais and everyone at Black Moss Press, Heidi and Dale Jacobs, Marie Jeannette, Dawn Greene, Rachel & Isabel Wing, Karl Szaefer, and Alice B. Toklas.